30 Days To $1K

Learn How to Minimize Your Expenses, Eliminate Your Debt and Build Your Savings

Adam Carroll

Dedication

This book was written on two very long flights across the U.S., prompted by a conversation with someone who was having trouble saving enough for an emergency fund. I hope you find this useful, helpful, and entertaining all at once!

It's dedicated to all of the students and recent graduates I've had the privilege of mentoring through the years. You are the reason I do what I do.

30 Days To $1K is also dedicated to my wife, Jennifer, without whom I wouldn't know half of what I do about saving, investing, and building a BIG life.

And, to my children who are the greatest adventure I've ever undertaken. I'm exceptionally proud of each of you!

Table of Contents

30 Days to Controlling Your Finances

If you constantly feel like your money is in control of you instead of the other way around, what you're about to read will skyrocket your ability to make, keep, and invest money to create financial freedom.

If you give me 10-15 minutes of your time for the next 30 days, I guarantee you'll have added $1,000 to your bottom line...

Throughout this 'Financial Educator' book, you'll learn 30 HIDDEN secrets that will amplify your wealth, payoff debt, and create more CONTROL of your money.

Note: This IS NOT a get rich quick scheme.

Quite the contrary. Over the next 30 days you'll be taken through a step-by-step process of:

- Shedding expenses faster than "The Biggest Loser" contestants shed weight!
- Cutting hidden fees like a laser beam through a cheese log!
- Negotiating better deals by using scripts that bring decision makers to their knees!
- Tracking your impulse purchases to alter

your "spendie" programming!

- Liquidating lazy assets to make your money work harder than you!
- And so many more ways to gain control, it would blow your mind if I gave them all to you here...

Getting control of your money is really very simple. The problem that most people have is they think it's going to take them a really long time, or they will have to totally curb their spending, or go on a budget, or live on a steady diet of dill pickles and velveeta cheese.

I say, NOT SO!!

In reality, you'll do one (maybe two) very minor actions each day that will progressively get you closer to ULTIMATE MONEY CONTROL and having a cool thou in the bank within 30 days (or so).

And the best part is... I'LL HOLD YOUR HAND THE WHOLE WAY.

I wouldn't send you down an unbeaten path in the dark of night. I'm sending you down a well-worn, oft-travelled path in the noonday sun with the skills, secrets, tips and tricks of thousands of people who've gone before you and have come out with solid finances and never-before-experienced security.

Each day is a new to-do. Some days you may be required to make a couple of calls, other days you may have to comparison shop services, and on occasion I may ask you to do something completely off the wall. (Those days are REALLY fun!)

And within 30 days, you will have more control than you've ever had before with your money. You'll know exactly where it's going, where it's coming from, how much you need to live on, how much you have in savings, where to legitimately cut costs, and on and on and on.

Think back to a time when you felt amazing about your money situation -- THAT'S EXACTLY HOW YOU'LL FEEL AFTER THIS COURSE!

And that's really what this is ... it's a course and I'm your instructor. And the reason I'm qualified to be your instructor is I've come from a position of extreme debt and am now in a position of extreme wealth.

I teach people from all over the country how to play the money game to win, and now I'm going to do the same for you one-on-one.

It's not uncommon for me to charge $3,500 or more

for an hour of my group training; but you get my instruction at a SIGNIFICANT discount.

My friends all think I'm crazy -- they think someone is going to steal the idea and charge 10X what I'm charging. They're convinced that I have to charge 3 or 4 times the amount for anyone to take the information seriously. They're convinced that I'm leaving thousands of dollars on the table per year!

And you know what? They're right.

But I believe in the average American's ability to get ahead so much that I'm willing to leave money on the table in order to make sure there's more in YOUR bank account.

While I could charge between $297 and $397 for the "coursework" that I'll be providing to you within this book, the actual investment you'll make in your own financial contentment is the cost of a cup of coffee.

It's that simple. I believe in you. I believe in your ability to rapidly pay off debt. To build a reserve account faster than you ever thought possible. To rid your life of stress and strife and excuses, and to finally experience what the wealthy do -- financial contentment.

So before you make a decision to invest in yourself, let me ask you:

Are you financially content?

Are you at a point in your life where money concerns are a distant memory and you've got your future mapped out entirely before you? If not, why not?

Is it that you:
- Grew up in a family where "there were things more important than money"?
- Have an abusive relationship with money (i.e. you abuse it!)?
- Are afraid of taking a hard look at your finances?
- Would rather be an ostrich with your head in the sand?
- Know that you've gotten screwed in the past and are afraid?
- Had a bankruptcy or foreclosure recently?
- Had a major life event recently? (death, birth, graduation, marriage, etc)
- Are "bad" with money?

If you're any of the things listed above (or anything else for that matter) but are ready to take a stand and control your money like an evil dominatrix, it's time to take action.

The 30 Day to 1k Financial Contentment course begins immediately and the first week will put you on the path to putting away a significant amount of money. In fact, if you follow the directions of all 30 days and you haven't put away $1,000 (or found at least $1,000 in expense savings) then I'll gladly refund your purchase fee.

It's really that simple.

Let me reiterate, the lessons we'll be going through in the book aren't super time intensive. On average, each lesson will take you about 10-15 minutes to complete. Some lessons, significantly less.

But it's the seemingly simple, insignificant tasks I give you that will net significant returns to your bottom line.

So let's get started. Turn the page to grab your your first assignment. It's an easy one, but an important one. And, it's the beginning of a month long love affair with saving money, eliminating debt, and increasing your financial I.Q.

Are you ready to get your wealth on? Good. I thought you were.

Turn the page to begin The 30 Days to 1k "Financial

Contentment" Course.

Chapter 1
Where's My Money?!

:: LESSON 1

Give yourself a pat on the back for investing in something that will truly make a difference in your life!

Before I give you your first assignment, I want you to commit to following the assignments EVERY day for a month without fail. Each assignment will vary in length, difficulty, and nature of task, but each is instrumental in YOU getting control of your money, and ultimately achieving financial contentment.

So, put one hand on your heart and the other on your purse or wallet and repeat after me:

"I, [your name], do solemnly swear to follow the lessons of The 30 Day to 1k Financial Contentment Course for a full 30 days. I agree to do the tasks asked of me willingly, knowing that they will ultimately lead to the control of my money, financial contentment, and a life free of money worries."

Did you read it aloud? If you're sitting around other people, MAKE SURE THEY HEAR YOU! They may be your best source of accountability -- and just may want to take the course with you.

Alright, let's begin lesson #1. The most obvious fact that comes with being in debt is that you're probably spending more than you make. Maybe you've had unforeseen expenses pop up, or you had to put holidays or birthday gifts on credit, whatever the reason you'd like to make up for your debt, the bottom line is, your expenses are out of whack with your income.

So, while this may seem trivial and insignificant, remember every task is significant and will lead to more and more wealth creation, more control of your money, and more financial contentment.

First task -- go find a small spiral bound notebook that you'll keep with you everywhere you go for the next two weeks. You can either buy one at the store (don't spend more than $1), find one swimming around your junk drawer, hiding at the bottom of your purse or briefcase, or in your kids' coloring book drawer. Wherever you get one, just make sure that you keep it on your person for the next two weeks.

Ok, go find one. Then come back and I'll tell you what to do.

You got it?

Good.

Now, number the pages of the little spiral bound notebook from today's date through the next two weeks. Each day should have the date at the top of a separate page.

What you're going to do with this notebook is write down everything you spend money on, regardless of how large or how small. If it's an 89 cent pack of gum, write it down. $1.25 for a can of coke? Write it down. Every gas fill-up, every lunch or dinner out, every cup of coffee, every check written for a bill. If you spend money on a given day, I want you to write that amount down, no matter how you spent the dough.

Debit cards, credit cards, checks, cash, pocket change, lint and gum, whatever! Just write the amount down and the method of payment every day for the next two weeks.

It should look like this:

Jan 1:
Credit Card $2.79 latte
Cash $.75 soda
Debit Card $9.79 Applebee's lunch

Jan 2:
Debit Card $32.00 gas
Credit Card $67.00 Gap

Jan 3:
Check $1075.00 mortgage
check $45.00 water bill
Cash $.75 soda

So that's it, I'll let you know what we're going to do with the data once the two week period is up. Until that time, just make sure that you're documenting EVERYTHING you spend money on!! EVERYTHING!!

Your Mission!

For Chapter 1, your mission is to find a spiral bound notebook, date the pages with today's date right through for two weeks and record everything you purchase.

Remember, it should look something like this:

Jan 1:
Credit Card $2.79 latte
Cash $.75 soda
Debit Card $9.79 Applebee's lunch

Jan 2:
Debit Card $32.00 gas
Credit Card $67.00 Gap

Jan 3:
Check $1075.00 mortgage
check $45.00 water bill
Cash $.75 soda

Chapter 2
Save/Save

:: LESSON 2

Hey, you 'showed up' for Chapter 2 of this book. Nice work. (I'm a big believer of positive reinforcement!)

So you should have in your possession a small spiral bound notebook that you're writing down all of your spending in for the next two weeks. If you didn't get that done yet, I'm giving you two assignments in this chapter -- first one -- GO GET A SMALL SPIRAL BOUND NOTEBOOK!

Don't trick yourself into believing that you can write it on a post-it, or your planner, or keep it in your phone. You won't do it! Make sure you're carrying that notebook with you everywhere and write EVERYTHING down that cost you anything!

Alright, Chapter 2 of the book is all about setting yourself up for financial success. One of the reasons that you may not have a ton of money in your savings account is because you don't have a savings account set up for savings!

Instead, what you set up when you opened your bank accounts was a "put-and-take" account. You put a little bit in and take a lot out.

Believe me, you're not alone in doing this.

Most people have just never identified one account as a save/save account. It's called save/save because that's what it's for. It's for savings and that's it!

So, this chapter's assignment is very simple and straightforward. You're going to open an account for save/savings that you're going to name any of the following:

[Your name's] Go To Hell Fund
[Your name's] Emergency Account
[Your name's] Rainy Day Someday Account
OR
[Your name's] Financial Contentment Account

And where might you open this account? I'm going to tell you. Actually, I'm going to give you a couple of options, and direct you to the one that I like right now.

The account that you're setting up is going to be a high-interest money market savings account.

(A money market account is simply a savings account on steroids, and in this case, NOT a part of your existing bank.)

There are three companies that I really like who are offering high interest money market savings accounts. In no particular order, they are:

- www.smartypig.com
- www.emigrantdirect.com
- www.ingdirect.com

There are pros and cons of each, but for now, the one I most like is SmartyPig. It's a refreshing way to save and the service allows you to specify how much you'd like to put away and then it will break down how much per month you need to save to hit your goal.

You can also email your friends and family and tell them what you're saving for and they can contribute to your account electronically. It's pure genius and the guys behind the company are insanely creative. Plus, they're paying more interest than almost anyone online.

The reason that I'm encouraging you to set up an online money market savings account is two-fold:

#1: Because these companies don't have huge brick and mortar buildings and expenses, they're more able to keep costs low and returns high.

#2: Because it's not tied directly to your bank, you're going to be less likely to spend the money in the account.

So, your mission, (and you will choose to accept it), is to set up an account with one of the above three. They are all reputable -- I have accounts with each. And, each one can be linked to your existing checking and savings accounts to make the transfer of money extremely easy.

Now get to it! Pretty soon, saving money will be as easy as fishing with dynamite.

BOOM!

Your Mission!

For Chapter 2, your mission is to set up a money market account with one of the following three companies:

1. www.smartypig.com
2. www.emigrantdirect.com
3. www.ingdirect.com

Make sure you give it a name, something like:
[Your name's] Go To Hell Fund
[Your name's] Emergency Account
[Your name's] Rainy Day Someday Account
OR
[Your name's] Financial Contentment Account

Chapter 3
Credit Report 101

:: LESSON 3

(To the theme of *Welcome Back, Kotter*)

Welcome back, welcome back, welcome back...

This chapter is a very easy assignment, and one that will blow your mind if you've never had a chance to see what I'm going to tell you to do.

The first week of the Financial Contentment Course is all about gathering information and getting set up for financial success, well-being, peace of mind, and Ultimate Contentment.

Here's a question: What's something that nearly every person in America has or will have at some point, but rarely sees? (and no, it's not a big posterior, but good guess.)

Do you give up?

IT'S A CREDIT SCORE!

For me to explain how your credit score is

calculated would require advanced degrees in calculus, statistics, and advanced ergonomic design.

Suffice it to say, your credit score is calculated by an algorithm that was written specifically for each individual credit bureau.

There are three main ones and they are:
1. Experian
2. Trans-Union
3. Equifax

The information that's collected on your credit report comes from the "tradelines" or accounts that you've opened with credit providers like Capital One, MBNA, The Gap, Victoria's Secret, The Home Depot, Ford Motor Credit, etc.

Each of these creditors reports your payments (or lack thereof) every single month and the payment history becomes a (relatively large) part of your credit score.

The other elements of your credit score include:

- Balance to Limit ratios (how much of your credit limit you're spending)
- Payment History
- Length of Credit History

- New Credit
- Inquiries

Now you've probably seen the freecreditreport.com commercials playing on TV, but don't believe the hype. The credit report you'll end up getting will NOT be free. In fact, this company is owned by a guy who's made a fortune in the lead generation business. The information you're paying him to see (remember I said it's not free), will eventually be sold to people in the mortgage business, car business, life insurance business, and other very salesy industries.

If you want a truly free credit report, the ONLY place to get one is at www.annualcreditreports.com. This is the ONLY government sponsored website where the reports you get are truly free.

Here's the catch. You'll get a credit report from this site—in fact, you can order one from all three different bureaus listed above. But, you won't get your score. To see your score will cost you $5.

Why do they charge for it? I have no idea.

The most important part about pulling your credit report is making sure there isn't anything that's reporting in error. If you've got erroneous information, outdated information, or accounts that you don't recall signing up for, it's wise to challenge the information.

The Fair Credit Reporting Act says that anything that's reporting in error (or believed to be) has to be verified as accurate or it has to be removed within 45 days.

So, here's the most important part of this task (which I'm about to give you)...

I want you to pull a credit report from one or two (or all three) of the bureaus that are available on the website directly above. Go through all of the tradelines and make sure that what you see is accurate to the best of your knowledge. If it isn't correct, then challenge the information by writing a letter to the creditor and let them know that the information listed is not accurate.

The reason this task is so important is so much of your financial life is based on what your credit score is. In a nutshell, the higher your score, the lower the interest rate you'll pay on your car loans, credit cards, mortgages, insurances, and any other revolving account that you may open.

Disregard your credit score and you may just pay twice as much for nearly everything in your life. Paying close attention to your credit report and scores will save you a bundle over time (especially in Week #4!).

So, the task is to log onto www.annualcreditreports.com, order the report from one, two, or all three bureaus and review for misinformation.

The reason you'd order all three is quite often the information is correct on one report and wrong on another. It's really more of a precaution.

The reason you wouldn't order all three is you're only allowed one copy per bureau per year for free. So what I generally recommend is order one report every 4 months from the next credit agency on the list.

The next lesson is going to get to the heart of the matter and you'll learn how to knock your credit card debt out like Buster Douglas did Mike Tyson!

Your Mission!

For Chapter 3, your mission is to log onto www.annualcreditreports.com, order the report from one, two, or all three bureaus and review for misinformation.

Here's those bureaus again:
1. Experian
2. Trans-Union
3. Equifax

Chapter 4
Tracking

:: LESSON 4

At this point in the course, you're starting to pick up what I'm laying down. You know my sense of humor, you know I've got your back, and you can absolutely trust in what I'm about to show you.

Some time ago, I had close to $8,000 in credit card debt. The debt was spread over 4 or 5 cards and each had significant interest rates, so my ability to knock them out was extremely limited.

Or so I thought...

I invested $200 in a course that taught me everything I needed to know to pay the debt off rapidly and I'm about to share the same (and now advanced) information with you. (By the way, I knocked out my debt in just under 10 months using the information I'm sharing with you. And I was making less than $35,000 a year at the time.)

Remember I said that Week #1 is all about information and then what we do with the information will really kick in during Weeks #2 and

#3? Well, this week's assignment is figuring out just how much you owe and what the interest rates are on each credit card (or any other tradeline, liability, or debt you're carrying).

The link below goes to a spreadsheet, that's available to anyone, that helps determine what the fastest route to paying off your debts might be.

http://www.vertex42.com/Calculators/debt-reduction-calculator.html

Your task for this chapter is to fill in all of the information from your credit report that you got from the last assignment; to the spreadsheet that you'll download from the link above. Make sure you contact the companies that have issued these credit cards, car loans, etc. and find out what the interest rate is on each. That will be a critical part of our next step and the negotiation of rates in the next week or two.

So, to recap, your task is to click on the link above, download the spreadsheet, and fill in all of the information that you received from the credit reports. (Balances, minimum payments, interest rates, etc.)

What this spreadsheet will do is show you in which order you should be paying off your debts. You see, most people with multiple accounts pay just a little bit more than the minimum on several accounts every month and dilute the effectiveness of the payoff process.

To give you an analogy, instead of hunting with a laser beam, you're hunting with a flashlight. It's just not as effective.

Instead, the downloadable form from above will tell you which liability you should be focusing your attention and any available cash on. There are two methods of figuring out which debts get eradicated first. Either the ones with the highest balance, or the ones with the highest interest rate.

From a purely psychological perspective, you'll have more satisfaction and fulfillment seeing debts paid off in full, so it makes sense that you'd pay off the lowest debts first, no matter what the interest rate.

Once a debt is paid off in full, the payment you'd been making on it is simply rolled to the next debt until it is taken care of. Those payments are then rolled up to the next debt and so on.

The idea is you're sending more than the minimum payment to one debt in particular until it is blasted away while all of the other debts ONLY get minimum payments and not a dime more.

Remember, you want to take a financial laser beam to your debts to blast them to smithereens.

So, for now, download and fill out that form and in the next lesson I will tell you what to do with the information that it provides (and how to kick debt's ass all over the block!).

Your Mission!

For Chapter 4, your mission is to download the spreadsheet and fill in all of the information that you received from the credit reports. (Balances, minimum payments, interest rates, etc.)

Find the spreadsheet here:
http://www.vertex42.com/Calculators/debt-reduction-calculator.html

Chapter 5
Fee Elimination

:: LESSON 5

Hey you, welcome to Chapter 5, the day we tell your bank to take their fees on a long walk off a short pier...

One of the largest revenue sources for banks these days is fee-based revenue. These fees didn't exist to the extent they do today and it's a multi-billion dollar revenue stream for banks around the world.

Here's what I find most interesting—people have no clue that they're being charged the fees. They're completely astonished when I tell them to look closely at their bank statements and see what kind of crazy fees are being charged. It's nothing to see $35-$40 charged for overdraft fees, a 10% fee for direct deposit advance, a $75 annual account holder fee, not to mention the $2.50 fee every time you use an ATM machine not in their network.

One of my clients even realized she was charged a fee when she deposited cash into her account! NOW THAT'S RIDICULOUS ... and guess what, she's not at that bank anymore.

The purpose of this chapters lesson is simple—we are going to eliminate any unnecessary fees on your account (and that includes insufficient funds fees, or NSF's).

Your task is to log onto your bank's website and print out the last 3 months worth of statements.

If your bank doesn't have online access or they charge you to look at past month's statements, CHANGE BANKS NOW! You want to make things easier on yourself, not harder...

Okay, when looking at your bank statements, there is usually a line-item on the statement that tells you when the bank has charged you a fee. It may be a usage fee, a direct deposit advance fee, an ATM fee, an "account" fee, or some other creative fee. Basically, anything on your statement that looks out of place I want you to circle in red.

Next, call your bank's customer service line and ask who has the authority to reverse fees charged on an account. If it's the person that answered, then talk to them, if it's a manager, then request to speak with the manager.

Making sure that you're keeping your calm, politely explain to the manager that you were reviewing your statement and noticed that you were charged $__ and you didn't realize that the bank charged you for that service. (If it's for an NSF, just let them know that this is not a regular occurrence for you and you'd like the charge reversed.)

Then politely ask, "The reason I'm calling is I'd like to have that charge reversed. Can you please do that for me?" (THEN BE QUIET UNTIL THEY AGREE.)

If the bank isn't willing to reverse charges, simply let them know that there are plenty of banks and credit unions available that don't charge those kinds of fees and you'll be switching to one of them. More often than not, they'll back down and credit you the fee.

What we're shooting for is a free account. No crazy fees, no hidden charges.

Let me address the issue of overdrafts real quick—you know that the reason you're getting overdraft notices is you have no idea how much money is in the account at any given time. I'm not going to drill the notion of balancing your check-book in your head, but we are going to discuss your habits of writing down what you spend.

(You thought I forgot about that assignment, didn't you? On the contrary, that assignment is going to

keep rearing its ugly head, so make sure that you're writing down EVERYTHING you buy for the next 9 days!!)

I recently saved a couple of clients over $1,200 a year in bank fees. They were in a Direct Deposit Advance (DDA) account which advanced them $500 from their direct deposit paycheck 5 days before they were to receive the check from their employer. The bank charged a 10% premium every time the advance occurred—a $50 fee every two weeks!

The way the bank had set up the account, the advance happened no matter if they needed it in their account or not. The total APR of this program is 120%—and you thought 34.99% on a credit card was bad!

One of the two greatest expenses we have in life is the interest expense on debt (the amount of money we spend to borrow money).

In the next chapter we'll tackle how to minimize that as well.

You're doing great! Keep it up!

Your Mission!

For Chapter 5, your mission is to log onto your banks website, grab your last three bank statements and circle anything in red that looks like a bank charge or that you're not sure about.

Then follow these steps:

1. Call your bank's customer service line and ask who has the authority to reverse fees charged on an account. If it's the person that answered, then talk to them, if it's a manager, then request to speak with the manager.

2. Speaking calmly, politely explain to the manager that you were reviewing your statement and noticed that you were charged $___ and you didn't realize that the bank charged you for that service.

3. Politely ask, "The reason I'm calling is I'd like to have that charge reversed. Can you please do that for me?" (THEN BE QUIET UNTIL THEY AGREE.)

If the bank isn't willing to reverse charges, simply let them know that there are plenty of banks and credit unions available that don't charge those kinds of fees and you'll be switching to one of them. More often than not, they'll back down and credit you the fee.

Chapter 6
Car Refinance

:: LESSON 6

I'm gonna make this one easy on you.

If you own your car outright, you get to 'skip' this chapter.

If you have a loan against your car, read on...

This chapter's task is calling the bank that's holding your car loan and finding out what the interest rate is.

Then it's up to you to do a little research. Depending on your year, make, mileage and model AND how much you currently owe, it may be possible to refinance your car loan with a local credit union at a significantly lower rate.

I'm talking like 10% lower or more.

You see, when you go buy a car and you trust the salesperson's finance department to find you the "best deal", they never do. Instead, they figure out what they want to make on you and give you whatever interest rate makes them the most money (I'm painting with a broad brush, but it's generally true).

They more than likely asked you, "well, what do you want your payment to be?" And then they work backwards into the rate to figure out how many years they can finance you to get you that payment. At 4.9%, you might have a 3 or 4 year loan. At 19.9%, you might have an 8 or 9 year loan for the same payment, it will just take you twice as long to payoff and cost twice as much.

So, your research is to Google 'Credit Union Car Loans' in your area and see what interest rates come up. Then call the two or three lowest rate places and tell them about your car, your current loan, and that you'd like to save money if possible.

If they say they can help you refi, then get on it! You might just save yourself $20-$50 a month and a couple thousand in interest over the life of the loan.

If they can't help you due to mileage, age, what you owe, etc. then we'll talk about how to payoff the car loan faster in the next couple of weeks.

So far, you're doing great. I know it seems like we're covering a lot here -- just trust me when I tell you the next two weeks will be enormously rewarding for you. We're just doing the legwork now that will lead to money in the bank!

The next lesson is going to be fun. And eye-opening...

Your Mission!

For Chapter 6, your mission is to Google 'Credit Union Car Loans' in your area and see what interest rates come up.

Call the two or three lowest rate places and tell them about your car, your current loan, and that you'd like to save money if possible.

If they say they can help you refinance, then get on it!

Chapter 7
Spending Plan!

:: LESSON 7

Hey there!

Did you get anywhere with the car loan? I sure hope you found someone willing to get you into a lower car loan rate. If not, we'll do a little credit fixin' over the next 3 weeks and then you can go back and try again. Don't fret, we'll get there soon.

In this chapter, I'm not going to have you call anyone, but I am going to call you out!

If you're anything like me (and I'm guessing you are cuz you're in my course), you hate the 'B' word. You know the one ... budget. Uggh. It gives me hives.

Before I totally kicked my finances in the arse, I hated the word budget. It's so restrictive, isn't it? It has the same connotation as diet and no one likes those either. So, I started to call my budget my SPENDING PLAN!

Yeah, that sounds so much sexier because I like to spend money ... I don't like to diet.

So, this chapter's assignment is going to be fun. You're going to create a spending plan. This plan doesn't have to be ultra-involved and in fact you'll find a copy of the spending plan form you'll be using http://www.vertex42.com/ExcelTemplates/ monthly-household-budget.html. All you have to do is download it and fill it out (in Excel), or print it out and use it as a hard copy.

The beautiful thing about this spending plan is it will tell you if you need to reduce some of your spending. As you plug numbers in for groceries, rent, utilities, diapers, etc., the spreadsheet will tell you if you have positive disposable income or negative disposable income.

Positive ... good. Negative ... bad (use your George Bush voice, it sounds funnier).

And ultimately, what we're striving for throughout the next 30 days is to reduce your expenses, reduce your debt, and increase your disposable income so that you can:

a) save more, and
b) have more financial contentment, which comes from not having crazy financial pressures all the time.

Savvy?

Good. (And becoming more so, I might add.)

So get going. Download the form, enter in what you think the numbers are that you spend in each category. You'll notice at the top is where you plug in your after-tax (take home) income. This is what allows the spreadsheet to determine what your disposable income percentage is.

We're shooting for 10% or more in disposable income. If you're less than 10% (or even negative) then we've got some serious work to do.

If you're over 10%, but you have little to nothing in savings, then the small spiral bound notebook from Chapter 1 will tell us everything we need to know in the next several days!! :)

(YOU ARE STILL WRITING DOWN WHAT YOU SPEND, RIGHT?!)

The reason I'm having you do this now is we're going to compare what you think the amounts are and the actual amounts. Then, we're going to do some hard core expense reduction and all the money you save is going to your debt elimination laser beam.

I'm gonna have you debt free and dancing a jig before you know it!

Go ahead, practice the dance for me ... woooo! I like it.

The next chapter task is going to freak you out it's so good. It will be like opening the door to abundance and prosperity and greeting them like old friends.

Did someone say "Financial Contentment party?"

Rock out with your stock out!

Your Mission!

For Chapter 7, your mission is to download the form, enter in what you think the numbers are that you spend in each category.

http://www.vertex42.com/ExcelTemplates/monthly-household-budget.html

The right hand side at the top is where you plug in your after-tax (take home) income. This is what allows the spreadsheet to determine what your disposable income percentage is.

Chapter 8
Abundance

:: LESSON 8

This chapter begins one of my favorite weeks of all times. It's abundance week!

First and foremost, we have to do this cuz I'm feeling a lack of energy around getting control and we gotta have energy for this week.

So, put one hand on your heart and the other on your purse or wallet and repeat after me:

"I, [your name], do solemnly swear to follow the lessons of The Financial Contentment Course for a full 30 days. I agree to do the tasks asked of me willingly, knowing that they will ultimately lead to the control of my money, financial contentment, and a life free of money worries."

Now shout out to someone around you, "I'm really gonna do it!" (It can be a person, dog, cat, tree, whatever...)

So the reason I love this week is because when I got to this step in my debt elimination phase (way back before I developed the course), I never imagined how much the next 7 days could change my life.

You have no idea what you're in for...

Let me give you a hint -- you are about to become a peddler in the marketplace.

There is a philosophy called Feng Shui. It's the whole notion that there is energy in everything around us and that energy can become blocked by "stuff". So, we're gonna release a whole lotta great money energy at your place by getting rid of all the stuff that has clogged up your financial house for so long.

Everyone (and I mean everyone) has more stuff than they really need. It's not as if people go out to spend a fortune on trinkets, trash, clothing, shoes, belts, purses, CD's, DVD's and furniture. They do it over time, little by little.

And then one day they wake up and have a rental storage facility full of "stuff" they haven't seen in a year but they've spent $50 a month keeping it there.

Say it with me, "Duh".

So, in this chapter you're going junk collectin'. And over the next several chapters, I'm gonna teach you how to move it quickly, profitably, and in the process, rid yourself of junkitis forever. Oh yeah, and make cold hard cash.

It's gonna be beautiful.

Now the reason we're doing this in phases is it may be a tad difficult for you to part with some of your "treasures".... read, junk. I get it. It meant something to you at some point and that's why you kept it around. Take a freakin' picture of the thing and put it in a scrapbook!

I'm going to let you collect all the stuff that you think you can part with and put it in a room of your home. Anything that you absolutely can't part with, pull out of the pile. But go after this task with passion about shedding the stuff and unblocking the energy.

So, I just said that everyone has more stuff than they need. What they are holding onto are lazy, idle assets that are worth something to someone. You know that comforter you keep in the back closet that hasn't seen the light of day in months? That's probably worth $50 to someone. The dresser that's in the garage that may someday be refinished? Yeah, an antiques collector would probably pay you a pretty penny for it.

CD's and DVD's -- did you know there's a place you can sell them yourself online OR if you want to get rid of them quickly, just take them to <u>Half Priced Books.</u> You might not get as much, but you'll get something and they're now out of the house! (All of this we'll cover in the next couple of chapters...)

For now, what I want you to do is go through your house, your office, your basement, your attic, your storage facility, every closet and every cupboard and grab what you think is worth something AND what you are comfortable getting rid of. This includes clothing, shoes, purses, belts, tools, furniture, kitchen stuff, electronics, games, CD's and DVD's.

For the time being put this stuff in one room and display it like you're having a living room sale. You'll find out why tomorrow.

Keep this one thing in mind—if you're carrying credit card debt and you bought with credit the stuff we're selling, then you don't own it, it owns you. By doing all of this we are releasing the bonds of ownership this stuff has on you. Part of the reason people keep these lazy, idle assets is they are still paying much of it on their credit cards so they can't justify getting rid of them.

This task is as much psychological as it is practical.

And when you're done with this week, you'll feel like a Feng Shui Master with all the money energy swirling around you.

Feng yeah!

Now go get your stuff. (You're doing great! Keep it up!!)

Your Mission!

For Chapter 8, your mission is to go through your house, your office, your basement, your attic, your storage facility, every closet and every cupboard and grab what you think is worth something AND what you are comfortable getting rid of. This includes clothing, shoes, purses, belts, tools, furniture, kitchen stuff, electronics, games, CD's and DVD's.

Put this stuff in one room and display it like you're having a living room sale. Then head to Chapter 9 to find out what we're gonna do with it!

Chapter 9
Getting Rid of Stuff

:: LESSON 9

I peeked in your windows last night and my gosh, you have a lot of stuff to get rid of!

Actually, I was hoping there'd be just a bit more. I think you'll get so hooked on selling your merch' that you'll think about selling kids, pets, and more before we're all said and done.

You may be well-versed in hawking your goods, (they don't call you "The Garage Sale Master" for nothing) so I apologize if this information is beneath you. It's just that some people don't know how to go about getting rid of their lazy, idle assets.

We're going to start out slowly and progress into more technical ways of selling merchandise (i.e. selling online).

You no doubt have a fair amount of clothing that can be sold and/or donated. Our first attempt is going to be selling it and if that fails then even donating can help clear your Feng Shui energy and give you a nice tax deduction.

If you dug around in your significant others' closets for clothes, just make sure that he/she is okay with selling that favorite bowling shirt.

If you know of a consignment shop in your town, that's the first place to take your clothes. There are several locally owned shops in my town that sell high-end clothing that's lightly worn. Just look for 'clothing consignment' in the yellow pages or on Google.

Also, franchises like 'Once Upon A Child' are great for selling kids' clothing. Every season my wife takes the last round of clothes our kids grew out of and sells them on consignment or to OUAC.

If all else fails and no one wants your yellow plaid polyester jumpsuit, then donate it to Goodwill so some college kid has a Halloween costume for next year. Just make sure to keep your receipt so that you can take it as a charitable donation. (I'll cover the tax stuff in Week 4 -- it's highly advanced -- which is what you'll be by then!)

As we begin this week and you start by selling all of your family's clothing (kidding), just remember that ALL of the money made from the sale of your lazy, idle assets is going to pay down debt, build your Financial Contentment Fund (FCF), or BOTH!

So, before you go sell your stuff, write 'FCF' on an envelope and put all of the cash you receive in there! I'll tell you what we're gonna do with it in the next few chapters.

Just don't go shopping with it! NO MORE JUMPSUITS!

Your Mission!

For Chapter 9, your mission is to go through your clothing, your kids' clothing and your significant other's clothing and get rid of what hasn't been worn in 6 + months.

Look for a local consignment shop to sell them too, or give them away to a charity, making sure to grab a receipt to use later.

Chapter 10
Craigslist 101

:: LESSON 10

Once upon a time, there was this guy named Craig. He lived in a little apartment in San Francisco and he decided to put together a list for all the other San Franciscans. The list was sort of like an online classified ad and it spread like wildfire.

Now you can get anything you want in any area you want on Craigslist.com. (Including a date. Yikes.)

But a date is not what you're selling on Craigslist. You're selling lazy, idle assets and people will flock like geese to a koi pond when you post something for sale.

All of them with cash in hand.

If you've never done it before, the process of selling stuff on Craigslist could not be easier. In the upper right hand corner of the site, there is a link that says 'post an item.' When you click the link, it will ask you to select the category of the item you are posting. The category you post your wares in should be relatively obvious.

Craigslist allows you to post descriptions of the products, 4 photos, the location, and an email address to get in touch with you (which it will randomize if you're not comfortable with someone knowing your email address right away). It's not uncommon to list your phone number so interested parties can call you and ask you about the stuff for sale.

Don't be afraid of this process! If it weirds you out to have someone show up to look at your stuff, just make sure there's another person home when they come by. The major majority of people searching Craigslist are frugal, savvy shoppers that are just looking for a little bargain—and you're going to give them a bunch!

If you don't want to bite off more than you can chew, just list a few items that are a little bit bigger in size. The reason you're going to start off with the big stuff is you want to bring in as much as possible in the immediate term to build that FCF and to pay down debt! Once you catch the "sellin'-stuff" bug, you'll be into selling the smaller items too.

Trust me, there's psychology to all of this. Remember, FENG SHUI. LESS IS MORE!

So this chapter's task is simple -- choose 5-10 of

your larger items and get them listed on Craigslist.com in your area. You'll want to do something creative with the listing headline— something that will get you noticed. Try **BOLDing** the words or try a creative sales line like "Total Liquidation!"

The most work you'll do on this task is going to be taking pictures of your stuff to post on Craigslist. If you think just the text listing will do the trick, don't worry about the pictures, but the pictures almost always make a product sell that much faster.

If the product you're selling can be easily looked up on Google.com, type in the product in Google and click images. Then right click on the image of your product and select save image as ... to save the image to a Craigslist file on your desktop. (Oh yeah, put a Craigslist file on your desktop.)

Then, when it's time to post the items, you've already got the photos you need saved to your computer.

Badda Bing, Badda Boom.

While you ARE looking to make some money with this, you are NOT looking to sell this stuff at a premium or for more than you paid for it. You're purging these lazy idle assets from your home to make room for the abundance and wealth that is sure to come your way.

Now be nice to the people that come to the door with cash (you don't accept checks!), and put that money in your FCF as soon as it's in your grubby little hands!

Nice going, you!

Your Mission!

For Chapter 10, your mission is to choose 5-10 of your larger items and get them listed on Craigslist.com in your area.

Do something creative with the listing headline—something that will get you noticed. Try **BOLDing** the words or try a creative sales line like "Total Liquidation!"

Chapter 11
Clearing the Clutter

:: LESSON 11

Alright, now you're getting the hang of it! You're starting to sell the junk that's kept your money magnet blocked for so long and it's time to increase the polarity...

In this chapter, we're going through CD's and DVD's.

I can almost hear you already:

"But I might want to listen to those CD's someday!"

OR

"If I bought it, I must've really liked that movie and someday may watch it again."

If If's and But's were candy and nuts, oh what a Christmas it'd be!!

You spent 'IF-COME' on this CRAP! It wasn't income, it was if-come. That's why you're still financing your CD's and DVD's on your credit card (or if it isn't the CD's and DVD's that you're financing, it was buying them with the cash you did have that made you put meals, clothes, and whatever else is clogging up the plastic).

So, your task is simple. Round up every CD, DVD, VHS, 8-Track and cassette tapes and separate them out into an A, B, and C pile.

- The A's you will probably listen to or watch again.
- The B's are maybes and;
- The C's are definite goners.

Go back through the B's one more time and everything that you think you might want to keep, burn into iTunes so you have it for later. Then put that CD or DVD in the C pile—it's going bye-bye.

If you're feeling ambitious and want to list the CD's and DVD's online in an effort to get a little more money, go to www.half.com and list them there. It's incredibly easy to do. Half.com is an eBay company and one where people don't buy through auctions, they simply buy at a price that looks reasonable to them.

The key is when you list the items, there will be a chart that pops up telling you what the last purchase price was and the median sales price of that item historically. If you want to move it right away, price your stuff about 50 cents cheaper than every listing.

Yes, you're not getting as much as you maybe could, but you're guaranteed to move it much much faster than someone trying to get 50 cents more.

If you're all about getting the fastest buck for your stuff, then it's a better idea to take these items to a Disc-go-round, Half Priced Books, or some other reseller of "gently used" merchandise.

I've always found Half-Priced Books to be relatively fair in what they give for CD's and DVD's. Granted, they're in it for a profit, so you're not getting top dollar, but they will take just about everything you bring in (assuming it's in good shape). It's cash in hand as soon as they decide what they can give you.

So, get crack-a-lackin'. Some poor schmuck is just dying to get their hands on your Village People CD and your DVD copy of Pretty Woman.

Boo yah!

Your Mission!

For Chapter 11, your mission is to round up every CD, DVD, VHS, 8-Track and cassette tapes and separate them out into an A, B, and C piles.

- The A's you will probably listen to or watch again
- The B's are maybes
- The C's are definite goners

Go back through the B's one more time and everything that you think you might want to keep, burn into iTunes so you have it for later. Then put that CD or DVD in the C pile—it's going bye-bye. You could also do that with the A's if you wanted to.

If you're feeling ambitious and want to list the CD's and DVD's online in an effort to get a little more money, go to www.half.com and list them there.

Chapter 12
Sell it Like it's Hot!

:: LESSON 12

You are a selling machine!

In this chapter, I'm going to tell you a story and then give you a couple ideas on how to boost the dough you're making getting rid of stuff.

The story...

A buddy of mine named Jerry was obsessed with Nike Air Jordan tennis shoes. Like from the first pair to the last, he had every version of Air Jordans that Nike ever came out with. It seemed like the thing to do until he had 18 pairs of shoes in his closet that he couldn't bear to part with -- then it just seemed like a sickness!

Jerry wasn't overly adept at selling stuff on eBay, so he found an eBay reseller that would sell his "goods" and get paid a small commission for the service. They listed the shoes in lots and as individual pairs and were absolutely blown away by the outcome.

In 3 weeks, all 18 pairs of shoes had sold.

Did I mention these were worn shoes? Everyone say it with me ... eeeeeewwwww.

Not so gross was the total amount he made selling his sweat-soaked sneaks: $2,375!

SOME OF THE SHOES SOLD FOR MORE THAN THEIR PURCHASE PRICE!

If eBay-ing stuff isn't your bag, consider finding someone that could help you sell your stuff on eBay and collect a small fee for it. It's a great place to sell stuff if you know what you're doing.

If you don't know the strategies, the how-to, the writing of ads, then you might not get what you thought you would.

For some people, selling on eBay will come as second nature. If you have a healthy collection of something that needs to be sold, consider hiring an outside party to do it for you.

So, over the past four chapters, we covered selling clothes on consignment, lazy idle assets on Craigslist, CD's and DVD's at half.com, and smelly shoes on eBay. Savvy?

The point is, you're a selling machine now. When you want to buy something ... Anything ... it's a one in, one out policy. You have to sell something that will cover (or almost cover) the cost of the new item.

And for now, it's one out, one out. Keep selling...

Overspending is so 1998.

Your Mission!

For Chapter 12, your mission is to find items to sell on eBay. If you've got high-end items like Nike shoes, or collectible items that people will buy, eBay is the place to go.

If you're not confident with selling on eBay yourself, pay someone else to do it for you. Choose a reputable eBay reseller and have them take care of the whole shebang.

Chapter 13
Show me the Money!

:: LESSON 13

Alright, we're 13 chapters (or 13 days if you've been sticking to the daily guide) down in your quest for Financial Contentment, a $1,000 cushion, and rapid debt elimination.

Here's my only question: How are you feeling so far?

I know the process of eliminating the clutter is an intense one, so I'm going to give you a little breather this chapter. You deserve it IF you've been doing the tasks each chapter like I ask you to. And please understand, I know you've got lots going on outside this crazy little project, but it takes 21 days to form a habit and the habit you're forming here is going to put you on the path to making, keeping, saving, and investing a TON of money over the long haul.

But we've got to stay on the path and I'm going to continue giving you daily doses of AC to make sure you're doing what you're supposed to.

So your task is real simple:

Get out your FCF envelope and count how much glue is in there.

But here's the real deal behind this task -- don't just count the money, I want you to recognize and accept the money as a gift of abundance from where abundance wasn't coming before. Every one dollar, five dollar, ten dollar, and twenty dollar bill you have in that envelope is like a gigantic pat on the back and kick in the a$$ to keep going!

WHAT?! A hundred dollar bill? How'd that get in there?

Ooooohhhh, that feels good.

Now, put one hand on your heart and the other on your purse or wallet and repeat after me:

"I, [your name], do solemnly swear to follow the lessons of The Financial Contentment Course for a full 30 days. I agree to do the tasks asked of me willingly, knowing that they will ultimately lead to the control of my money, financial contentment, and a life free of money worries."

Now find something with your reflection in it and say, "YOU are on your way to financial freedom!"

Count your money again, then put it back in the envelope and I'll tell you where we go from here.

Here's a hint: it's a little more advanced and a way to accelerate what you're doing!

One more question—can you feel it? That feeling of immediate future financial success? It's almost palpable on my end.

Me likey.

Your Mission!

For Chapter 13, your mission is to count the dosh in your FCF envelope and pat yourself on the back for a job well done ... BUT only if you've been doing the tasks every single day!

Chapter 14
Selling to Profiting

:: LESSON 14

So you've been selling your stuff; you more than likely have a decent chunk of change in your FCF envelope, and if you don't, you soon will.

In this chapter, we talk about how to advance the selling to profiting.

A profit, generally speaking, is income minus expenses. The income that you're making is coming from selling your stuff. However, the expenses you incurred in obtaining the stuff may have been higher. That's not profitable.

But, what if you were buying someone else's rejected stuff and then reselling on Craigslist or eBay for a profit? It works best on Craigslist because people are generally willing to negotiate on the purchase price of whatever they have out there.

As an example, our neighbor looks for high quality, name brand home furnishings that she can negotiate the seller down on and then turns around and marks the products up to resell on Craigslist.

She often reposts the goods the same day the other persons' ad came down. And most of the time, she sells the stuff for $20-$50 higher than she paid for it!

A caller I had on a radio show one day said he bought bulk quantities of PowerBars and sold them on eBay for a 150% markup. His only complaint was not being able to find bulk quantities of the bars to sell consistently. Did you catch that? The demand is there, but he lacked the supply!

There is a great site found at www.etsy.com. This is a site for people who like to sell handmade jewelry to people looking to buy unique one-of-a-kind items. And there are people absolutely cleaning house.

Consider what it might take to turn a profit on some of the goods you're seeing on sites like Craigslist, eBay, and Etsy.

The bottom line is, you're in debt, or without savings, or behind on bills because you may not be using everything you have to get everything you can get. And by "get" I don't mean buying. I mean making money.

Your task is this -- put on your entrepreneur hat and

think about how you might be able to make some extra money to put away, pay down debt, and build that Financial Contentment Fund.

- Can you sell others' stuff at a higher cost?
- Can you find a product that you can buy cheap and resell at a mark-up?
- Can you make products to sell on specialty sites?

If this is foreign to you, don't force it. I want the entrepreneurial bug to hit you between the eyes, not put you down on your kneecaps. I'm not sure that makes sense, but, whatever.

You get the driftwood, right?

Cool.

I gotta level with you.

The next few chapters are going to blow your mind. I'm going to show you how to save so much freaking money on common expenses that you'll cringe when you add up how much you've been spending all this time.

Are you ready? Set?

Haha. False start. Turn the page to jump to the next

lesson.

Your Mission!

For Chapter 14, your mission is to put on your entrepreneur hat and think about how you might be able to make some extra money to put away, pay down debt, and build that Financial Contentment Fund.

- Can you sell others' stuff at a higher cost? Go to cragislist.com
- Can you find a product that you can buy cheap and resell at a mark-up? Go to ebay.com
- Can you make products to sell on specialty sites? Go to etsy.com

Chapter 15
Review Time

:: LESSON 15

Hey, remember in the last chapter I told you how we were going to save you a boatload over the next two weeks? That wasn't just a load of boat.

The reason that most people are behind the financial 8-ball, having no savings, no emergency fund, and enough credit card debt to choke a camel, is they have no idea what they're spending money on. It's as if they have selective memory about the expenses they incur on a daily basis.

The internal communication goes like this:

"Oh, I did good today, I just spent $3.78 on a coffee."

But they forgot they ordered $12 of whatever the latest fundraising scheme their co-workers kid is involved in, and they pitched in $6 for the ice cream cake for the going away party for what's-her-face, and they put $33 on their credit card for gas and a carwash (and a big soda!).

So it wasn't just $3.78. It was $54.78.

If that happens once a week, it may not be a big deal. For most people, this is every other day.

AND, this is why we've been keeping track of daily expenses for the past two weeks! (Well, WE haven't been keeping track, that was YOUR job!)

If you did keep track of all your expenses in that little notebook -- CONGRATULATIONS!

If you didn't, one of your tasks is to go into your online banking platform and print out all of the transactions for the last two weeks. Then go into your credit cards online systems and find out what you spent money on there as well. Estimate the cash you've spent as best you can.

This is where the rubber meets the road. You know how in Chapter 7 we did a Simple Spending Plan? Now we find out how close that is to the actual spending.

Add up all of the expense items for the past two weeks and put them into a few categories in a spreadsheet. (What they are is up to you and your spending habits.)

The categories will probably include:

- Food/Eating Out

- Gas
- Clothing
- Entertainment
- Supplies
- Misc
- Groceries
- Coffee
- Cell Phone
- Utilities

Now total up all of the spending for the past two weeks and multiply that number times two.

If you included your mortgage, utilities, cell phone, etc. in the total, then only double the expenses you'll likely have the second two weeks.

Let's face it, you're going to spend this money habitually throughout the month.

1. Do any of the numbers surprise you?
2. Anything sticking it's tongue out at you like a bratty 8 year-old?
3. Any expenses you just want to kick to the curb?
4. How about eating out? How much higher is that than you thought it would be?

At this point, it would be foolish of me to tell you

that you have to cut all of these in half or more and save every penny. It's not just foolish, it's unrealistic.

I want you to cut out 15% of all the expenses. That's it, just 15%. If that seems oppressive to your budget, do 10%.

And whatever that number is that you are comfortable with, take that amount out of your checking account and put it in your FCF Envelope.

This is just the start. Imagine that 15% growing every month until you hit your $1,000 goal. Once that happens (it WILL happen), then we go attack any debts like a vicious tiger on a debt only diet.

Being financially free from any debt is right around the corner. Stick with me. The bigger hits are coming in the next three chapters.

By the way, if you missed the task for this chapter, it was totaling up your spending and figuring out where you're spending more than you should be. Then take 15% of that amount and put it in your FCF Envelope.

I'm really proud of the job you're doing. Even if it's half-ass, I'm still super pleased that you're putting yourself in the right mindset to tackle this! That's half the battle.

TO THE BATTLEFIELD!

Your Mission!

For Chapter 15, your mission is to total up your spending and figure out where you're spending more than you should be. Then take 15% (or 10% if that's more comfy) of that amount and put it in your FCF Envelope.

Chapter 16
Insurance

:: LESSON 16

In this chapter I'm gonna take you through a walk in the park. What I'm about to show you could be some of the largest and most immediate savings you'll have throughout this 30 Day Financial Contentment book.

Everybody everywhere knows someone in the insurance business. It's just a given. And most people, once they select that ever-important advisor, believe that they are home and they never need to switch affiliations or price shop.

It's hogwash.

Insurance rates and fees change as quickly as gas stations change their price of gas. So what may have been a great deal a few months or years ago may be extremely high-priced compared to what you can now get on the open market.

All I'm sayin' is, we're going price shopping...

There are several different variations of insurance

that you may (should) have. The most apparent ones are home owners or renters, auto insurance, and life insurance. Some folks also carry an umbrella policy that protects their assets against something that doesn't easily fall into the other insurance "buckets."

We're going to start with auto and homeowners because these are the two that could have the greatest impact on your savings per month and your ability to put a big chunk into your FCF or pay down debt.

As a general rule, most auto owners are carrying a $500 deductible so that if they are ever in an accident that is deemed their fault, they'll have to pay the first $500 out of pocket and then the insurance company picks up the rest. If you have $1,000 in your emergency account and you can swing a higher deductible, you have the opportunity to save anywhere from $150-250 a year on your insurance premiums by raising the deductible to $1,000.

Boom! Instant savings!

On your homeowners insurance, instead of going to a name brand retail insurance company, consider calling an independent insurance agent or broker that can find the best possible deal for you through his/her many insurance suppliers.

I recently had my auto, homeowners, life, and umbrella policies re-quoted and the net savings to me was over $1,100 a year! AND I raised my life insurance coverage!

So your task is pretty simple: I want you to find an insurance broker in the phone book and call them to price out your policies. What they'll need from you is the following:

- Name and address
- Date of Birth
- Social Security numbers
- Value of the home
- Anything extra you'd like insured (valuables like jewelry, etc.)
- Car make and model
- VIN# from the windshield

From this information, a broker should be able to shoot you over a quote within the day of how much they can save you.

Then, it's up to you ... Well, what are you waiting for?! Make the change and save some money!

Then take whatever you saved (for the year) and

put that money in your FCF Envelope. I just added $1,100 to mine! Imagine how many Benjamins you could put in your envelope by making a couple of calls.

Get on it! (Should take you no more than 20 minutes total)

WoooHooo!

Your Mission!

For Chapter 16, your mission is to find an insurance broker in the phone book and call them to price out your policies. What they'll need from you is the following:

- Name and address
- Date of Birth
- Social Security numbers
- Value of the home
- Anything extra you'd like insured (valuables like jewelry, etc.)
- Car make and model
- VIN# from the windshield

Then take whatever you saved (for the year) and put that money in your FCF Envelope.

Chapter 17
Cutting Cell Phone Expenses

:: LESSON 17

While we're on the cutting expenses kick, you probably have something that's almost always close by, that most people would consider their most needed possession, and that vibrates in your pocket or purse several dozen times a day.

It's your cell phone. (What were you thinking?!)

Whichever cell phone plan you have, more than likely was the right one for you when you got it, but it may be overkill now that most companies allow you to talk to other same plan users and/or a select 10 friends for free.

There's a great website www.lowermybills.com. The site allows you to plug in the details of your current account on a number of different services (i.e. insurance, cell phone, long distance, etc.) and then it tells you what the best possible scenario for you might be.

After plugging in my info in to the site, I ventured into the Verizon Wireless store close to my house and asked if they would optimize my plan for me. In less than 10 minutes, the customer service rep decreased the number of minutes in my package, had me add a texting package for my wife as she had gone over her limit the past 3 months, AND lowered my monthly bill by over $20 in the process!

Your task is to optimize your cell phone plan. Just make a call to the customer service number for your carrier and ask someone to review the plan you're currently on. If there's a way to cut costs without sacrificing your current usage, do it.

Here's another suggestion—most cell phone companies allow you to select 5-10 numbers that you regularly call or that call you. Google now offers a service called Google Voice that allows you to set up a number that people can dial that rings right to your cell phone.

If you start giving out that number to all of the people that call you and set up your Google Voice number as one of your "favorites", you'll never be charged for minutes when people call you on that number. All calls received on your Google Voice
ill ring to your cell phone from that
T from the caller.

the cell phone companies. It's a
g. And I think there's an app and a

map for that.

Can you hear me now?

Good.

Your Mission!

For Chapter 17, your mission is to optimize your cell phone plan. Just make a call to the customer service number for your carrier and ask someone to review the plan you're currently on. If there's a way to cut costs without sacrificing your current usage, do it.

Remember to check out the site www.shrinkmybills.com before you call your carrier so you know what and where you could be saving on your plan.

Chapter 18
Quick and Painless Savings

:: LESSON 18

That cell phone thing from the last chapter was pretty cool wasn't it? Just think of how much money you'll be saving! It gives me warm fuzzies...

This chapter's cost savings measure is quick and painless. We're gonna set out to normalize the cost of your utilities and bring it down however we can.

First things first, almost all utility companies offer budget billing where they annualize your spending, divide that number by 12, and that's what you pay on a monthly basis. If you're not on this plan, you need to be. It allows you to adequately predict what your monthly utility cost is going to be and gives you something to shoot for in bringing it down.

Now here are the fastest and simplest ways to bring it down:
Call your local energy company and ask them to do an "energy audit". Most public service utilities will do this for free AND they'll bring you goodies like compact fluorescent lightbulbs (more energy efficient), hot water heater blankets, and on

occasion, they'll even install a programmable thermostat.

Don't overlook the smaller improvements as you get started on this warpath to cost efficiency. Even replacing incandescent light bulbs with CFL bulbs can create hundreds of dollars in savings per year.

Worn weather stripping can cause unnecessary furnace and A/C expenses, and outdated appliances can be more expensive than simply replacing them with energy efficient models.

There's a big push for all homes to be more "green" and quite often the tax credits you can get for energy efficient purchases will offset the cost and then some.

The programmable thermostat is a biggie. So many homes are heated or cooled throughout the day when no one is home. Stop that by programming when you're there and when you're not.

It's so cool to save money...

Your Mission!

For Chapter 18, your mission is to schedule an energy audit, buy a few CFL bulbs to replace your old energy hogs, and get on budget billing.

Chapter 19
Cutting Costs in Gas

:: LESSON 19

Alright, you're really in the thick of the cost cutting and extreme savings measures now!

Your task is also very simple—look at the amount of money you're spending in gas each month. If it seems high, this is where we're going to knock it down a peg or two.

There's a crazy phenomenon that I've been reading about called "hypermiling" where by paying attention to HOW you drive your car, you'll automatically improve your miles per gallon.

You can check out more for yourself at www.hypermiling.com. It's really pretty fascinating.

Tonight I want you to check the air in your tires and make sure they're properly inflated. Low tires can cause unnecessary fuel consumption.

Consider what trips you're making and where you can cut back. I'm not one to curtail all driving all-together just to save $30 a month, but I will try and bundle tasks together so I'm not racing all over town every day.

That was easy, wasn't it?

You've been working so hard, I just decided to give you an easier task, that's all.

Tomorrow is when you get your game face on and take on what might be your worst nightmare -- a call center employee! (Don't worry, I'll give you a script!)

It's going to save you a small fortune!

Guess what? I talked a friend of mine who loved her big Ford Expedition into down sizing into a sedan. She immediately cut $75 a month off her car payment and $100 a month from her gas bill. I'm just sayin'...

Your Mission!

For Chapter 19, your mission is to check out the site www.hypermiling.com. See if it's something that you can apply to your own driving.

Then I want you to check the air in your tires and make sure they're properly inflated. Low tires can cause unnecessary fuel consumption.

Figure out how you can save money on gas, you could even consider downsizing your car, if it makes sense...

Chapter 20
Cutting Back on Interest

:: LESSON 20

This chapter is going to be so much fun. Remember early on in this course I told you that the two greatest expenses we have, as individuals are taxes and the interest expense on debt? Well, we are going to tackle the interest expense on debt portion!

As you are probably aware, credit card companies rack up the majority of their profits in charging (in some cases) outrageous interest rates, penalties, and fees. What most people don't understand is those rates CAN be negotiated down. Particularly if you have been on-time in making the payments and you're currently in good standing with the card holder.

I just love messing with the call center folks who work for credit card companies. Here's what you have to know—most of the people who answer the phones are empowered to say NO but they are not empowered to say YES. So, your goal from the get-go is to get to someone with the power to say yes to whatever you ask.

Secondly, what you must also know is that most of the people in these call centers are also in some sort of debt dilemma. You'd think they'd know how to get out of it, but most are in exactly the same boat.

Thirdly, when you have an effective story about how you got in the position you are, or some explanation of your current lot in life (and you get someone sympathetic), they are much more willing to help you work out an effective solution.

So to recap, here are the three things to go into this call knowing:
1. The first, second, and maybe third person you talk to can only say no they cannot say yes. It's your job to bypass them and get to a manager.
2. The people you talk to are probably in the same boat. Don't rail on them, but on the credit card company.
3. Have a story or explanation as to how things got the way they did.

Alright, so if you are currently carrying any sort of credit card debt, this is the process we're going to go through:

1. Find out how much your total balance is and what your APR on the card is.

30 Days to $1K

2. Figure out how long you've had the card. (This should be on the credit report we pulled in Chapter 3 under 'Date Opened')

3. Call the 800# (toll free) listed on the back of the card and immediately ask to speak to someone in the *retention department*. The retention department are a little bit higher level folks who have the authority to lower the interest rates (though you still may need to ask for a manager).

4. Follow this script:

    - "Hi (say their first name), I was wondering if you could help me?

    - "I've been a customer of _____ for the past 5 years, always with a clean payment history though I've hit a bit of a speed bump in the past couple of months. While I'm doing everything I can to get caught up on my debts to you, because of some recent financial hardships, I'm calling to request a lowering of my interest rate to make the payments a little easier. What is the lowest you can bring my APR to in a situation like mine?" (Then shut your mouth tightly! Let them make an offer)

    - "Is that the lowest you can get it?"

    - "Is there someone else that has more authority to get it even lower? Can I talk to them please?"

Your goal is to get each and every card you have lower and lower until you're paying next to nothing in interest.

If you are carrying $5,000 in credit card debt and the APR is 20%, it's costing you $1,000 a year just for that debt! There's your FCF right there!

Stick to your guns throughout this process. I've heard stories of clients of mine that get the APR down to 0 percent for 12 months or more.

Keep this in mind as well -- credit card issuers are bleeding red ink right now because so many people are defaulting on their cards. They want to make sure that you continue paying, even if that means lowering the interest down to next to nothing.

So make a list of the cards you have, the numbers to call to request the lowering of interest, and put the script in front of you. IT WORKS!

Most people don't know they can call and request stuff like this. Ask and you shall receive.

While you're at it, why don't you call and ask if they'll reverse the late fees and annual fees on your account from the past 12 months. They might put another $100-200 back in your account just for asking.

You will succeed at this! Give it a go and stick to your guns!!

Debt sucks!

Your Mission!

For Chapter 20, your mission is to make a list of the cards you have, the numbers to call to request the lowering of interest, and put the script in front of you. IT WORKS!

Chapter 21
Lower Your Phone/Cable/Internet Bills

:: LESSON 21

Did you stick it to your credit card company? Man, I hope you really gave it to them -- I mean, took it from them, I mean ... you know what I mean.

Do you know what they call people that pay off their credit card balances in full every month?

Deadbeats.

That's what they're called in the industry. If you pay off your balance in full on a regular basis the industry folks call you a deadbeat because they can't make any money off of you.

Sounds pretty awesome to me. Let's be deadbeats ... to the credit card companies anyway.

On to another chapter of crushing your savings goals ... are you ready?

Since you dominated the call center folks in the last chapter and now it's just commonplace for you to serve up a hot dish of whoopass on your bills, let's tackle the phone company.

If you don't have a home phone, then we're going to take a similar tack on your cable or high-speed internet provider. (DirectTV, AT&T U-Verse, or whatever you have...)

There is something called Moore's Law, which was named after Gordon Moore who was the co-founder of Intel. Gordon Moore was the first to make the observation that transistors on integrated circuits doubled every 18 months.

Interesting, but not relevant, right?

It's actually relevant because all of the services that we pay for on a monthly basis that have technology behind them (phone, internet, cable, cellular), all of these are making radical improvements in their services thereby cutting the costs of said services.

As an example, it used to be a big deal to have fast dial-up service. Now, most people think only the cavemen had dial-up.

I digress.

The point of this chapter's exercise is you're going to call your telephone service provider (providing you still have a home phone) and ask them to review your bill and see if there is a more advantageous package you could be a part of.

I made one phone call to our telephone carrier which also happens to handle our high-speed internet in an attempt to get free unlimited long-distance. Not only did I get unlimited long-distance, but they also increased the speed of our DSL, AND decreased the bill by over $15 a month. ONE CALL.

If you're phone-less at home, I'm going to have you tackle the cable company. More than likely, of the 75-475 channels you currently have, you're only watching about 12 of them. Do you really need all of those channels that you're paying for?

Consider making the 'one call' and finding out what other packages are available and how much you can save each month.

And if your significant other gripes too much about not being able to watch Celebrity Rehab shows, remind them that only 8% of the wealthiest in America watch reality television compared to 82% of the poor. After all, watching the shows only feeds the celebrity's means of buying their addictions.

You dig?

Your mission: Save a bundle on your bundle.

Tell the phone rep that Gordon Moore told you to call. They will have no freakin' clue what you're talking about.

And that's how you pay the rent... (2 snaps).

Just like a celebrity.

Your Mission!

For Chapter 21, your mission is to call your telephone/cable/internet service provider and ask them to review your bill and see if there is a more advantageous package you could be a part of.

And, possibly reduce your television watching in the process!

Chapter 22
It's all About the Coupons!

:: LESSON 22

Happy happy, joy joy!

It's Chapter 22 (or Day 22 if you're following the daily plan...).

We're three full weeks in to making saving a habit and you are CRUSHING it! So proud of you for reading this book and being a part of the FCF fun.

Saving money is fun, isn't it? Sure, it's sometimes kind of like a Fear Factor, stick your face in a bucket of yuck and come out with a scorpion in your mouth fun. But, it's fun!

The reality is, if you can make saving money fun and somewhat game-like, you'll be more apt to make this a part of your normal routine.

Take my wife, for example.

I like to call her the Coupon Princess. (She was raised in the Coupon Castle by the Coupon Queen and the Free-Spending King.) She (Capital L) LOVES to save money and she's damn good at it. And unbeknownst to her, I'm gonna share some of her secrets...

When I tell stories about how we paid off almost $40k in high-interest debt in a little under 2 years, people assume that we had no fun whatsoever. NOT TRUE. We had more fun than Honey-Boo-Boo at Dunkin' Donuts!

But we made it a game. As an example, we're like normal red-blooded Americans who like to eat out every now and again. The only difference is we'd look for every opportunity to dine for free or for as little as possible. At the end of a very nice dinner, we usually had a tab of under $20.

How, you might ask?

Simply by googling for coupon deals at the restaurants where we wanted to dine, we almost always could find a BOGO offer (Buy One Get One -- seriously, tell me you knew that...) and it was usually for an entree of the same price.

Sometimes we would get a free appetizer with the purchase of an entree and we would just split it. For dessert, we'd hit the nearest Mickey D's or Wendy's for a little ice cream treat.

What can I say? I'm a cheap date. (She was my sugar momma at the time. Now, I'm her sugar daddy. Because turn-about is fair play.)

Here's your mission for Chapter 22: go find somewhere to dine, but don't pay full price. Attempt to feed at least two people for under $20. This is as much to show you that it can be done as anything, but it's also a bit of a reward for making it three full weeks.

Do you realize that saving money for you is now a habit? If you've been at this the entire time with me -- and why wouldn't you? This jazz is now hard-wired into your DNA. There's no stopping the inner saver!!

By the way—if people haven't told you that you're losing your mind, you're not telling enough people what you're up to. When we were filling in the debt hole we'd made for ourselves, we got absolutely ridiculed by our friends.

Guess who's calling whom for loans these days?

I tell them the First National Bank of AC is deposit only.

When you go out and dine at a local eatery, calculate what your total bill would've been without the coupon and then put that amount of cash in your FCF. Every time you do this, put the money away.

Last year, the amount was over $1,600 for us!

Let's put that number in perspective -- if you don't have $1,000 in emergency savings and you find yourself going out to eat at least once a week, just looking for BOGO offers could put the grand in the bank for you.

Eat, save money. Eat, save money.

Wash, rinse, repeat.

Easy cheesy, lemon squeezy.

Your Mission!

For Chapter 22, your mission is to go find somewhere to dine, but don't pay full price. Attempt to feed at least two people for under $20.

Some coupon sites you can check out are:

- www.groupon.com
- http://retailmenot.com
- http://coupons.com

Chapter 23
Purging 101

:: LESSON 23

Hi it's me! Your wake-up call to saving, investing, and making money!

Remember back in the old days (like 18 days ago), when we talked all about living on less and allowing more energy in your home by purging all of the stuff. Are you still doing that? I'm super curious how much you've sold and how much you've made off of those treasures.

We're back on a purge-kick, only this time you won't have to do any selling of any kind. This purge is of the subscription variety.

Statistics show that most households don't read 74% of what they subscribe to. (Keep in mind that 63.3% of all statistics are made up on the spot.)

I'm guessing that you're tossing at least a paper, and probably several magazines in the recycle bin every week having never read them.

Am I right?

How much are you spending in subscribing to magazines, newspapers, and other things that you never read?

I'll be candid with you—I'm a total sucker for great copywriting. I've subscribed to more financial newsletters than I can even list. It's bad. So, about twice a year I go through and unsubscribe to these, usually saving at least a hundred and sometimes more than a hundred bucks.

What are you subscribing to at home or at work that can be eliminated?

Newspapers, magazines, online subscriptions like Netflix or Hulu+, security system monitoring, a gym membership?

Before you threaten to disavow this program, I'm not telling you to cancel all of these if you're enjoying them. Please, by all means, I'm all about Netflix and the fact that I can stream Ghostbusters to my phone. (Don't judge.)

But if you aren't using the services, it's time to kick 'em to the curb.

Take a gym membership as an example. We enroll in gym programs because we have the best of intentions, but if you've gone multiple months without going to the gym, you're just holding onto the keychain tag membership ID to make yourself feel better.

No one will fault you if you cancel the membership, but keep the ID tag on your keychain. Problem solved.

I can give you a bunch of reasons why doing this exercise is a good idea:
1. You're wasting time (which IS money) and mental energy debating what you should do with these things.
2. Most of what is in newspapers is bad news.
3. Most of what is in magazines is just mental chewing gum.
4. Magazines are free at the library.
5. The Kardashians are idiots.

'Nuff said.

Your mission: Cancel, cancel, cancel. Then cancel some more. Add up the savings and put that in your FCF.

Then sing: *"The hills are alive, with the sound of saving..."*

Your Mission!

For Chapter 23, your mission is to figure out what you're subscribing to at home or at work that can be eliminated?

Newspapers, magazines, online subscriptions like Netflix or Hulu+, security system monitoring, a gym membership?

Cancel whatever you haven't used in over two months or more.

Chapter 24
Taxual Healing...

:: LESSON 24

Hello you! In this chapter and the next, you're going to get some taxual healing. (Did you see what I did there?)

The advice in this chapter works great if you're used to getting a tax refund check at the end of the year. To some people, it's like a forced savings plan and they look forward to it like a 6 year-old looks forward to a birthday at Chuck E. Cheese.

If that's you, and you can't imagine NOT getting that big check from Uncle Scam, continue doing what you've always done. Just make sure that you're putting some of that money away for bigger and better things—like your emergency savings!!

If you're open to a new way of thinking, I'm about to blow your face off in a good way.

When you get a big check from the IRS at the end of the year, it means that you've given the good ole USA an interest-free loan for much of the year. And while our Uncle can be good to us occasionally (though not recently), the penny-pinchers at the Internal Revenue Service do not pay a return on the money of yours that they've been using for the past 12 months.

In short, you could've been using that money to your benefit.

Many of the people I work with don't really know how to get more in their pay checks (thereby getting less back at tax time).

This is the way to do it, and the simple math behind how this works:
When you started in your job, you filled out a W-4 form. Every employee fills one out in order to get a W-2 at the end of the year. The W-2 lists how much you made, both gross and net (how much before taxes and how much after).

The W-4 can be a very confusing form to fill out because there are no concrete examples of how many dependents equals how much deducted. I've found most people put either 0 or 1 in the dependent categories.

If you put 0 or 1 in for dependents, you'll get the maximum amount withheld in taxes, and probably get a fairly decent size refund.

However, that's not the goal for you. We're looking to bump your pay checks up so that you can bank that $1,000 that we've been working towards all month.

Here's the simple math on dependents (and deductions) -- every dependent you claim is like taking $2,400 in income deductions. In fact, if you know that you have $4,800 in potential deductions every year -- things like mortgage interest, student loan interest, and the like—then you'd claim 2 on your W-4 form.

If it's something you're comfortable doing, bump the dependents info up one number just to see what the end result is both in your pay check, and your refund at the end of the year. You can change it anytime and this is usually done through your company's HR department.

If messing with this stuff freaks you out, consider running it through the IRS withholding calculator found here: http://apps.irs.gov/app/withholdingcalculator/.

Just to give you a little more motivation, way back in the old days when you weren't a saver (back in Chapter 1 or 2), I mentioned that the interest expense on debt was one of the greatest expenses in life.

Well, the other greatest expense in life is taxes.

In the next chapter, I'll go into how to save some money in taxes completely legally and ethically. They are the secrets of the rich and you're about to join the club.

Do you know the handshake?

Just kidding ... there's no handshake. It's more like a full-body sport hug.

It's how we roll.

Your Mission!

For Chapter 24, your mission is to review your tax and specifically, the dependent's you can claim.

Here's the simple math on dependents (and deductions) -- every dependent you claim is like taking $2,400 in income deductions. In fact, if you know that you have $4,800 in potential deductions every year -- things like mortgage interest, student loan interest, and the like—then you'd claim 2 on your W-4 form.

If messing with this stuff freaks you out, consider running it through the IRS withholding calculator found here: http://apps.irs.gov/app/withholdingcalculator/.

Chapter 25
Reducing Taxes

:: LESSON 25

"Heigh Ho, Heigh Ho, It's Off To Work I Go!"

Do you find yourself singing these words on your way in to your job?

I bet you would sing them if you were doing some work for yourself. In the last chapter, I mentioned me sharing some secrets to paying less in taxes legally and ethically, and working for yourself is the ticket.

There is a reason that the rich get richer, and part of the reason is they pay significantly less in taxes as a percentage of their income. And before you go on that tirade about it not being fair, it's actually defined in the tax code that you are legally required to pay exactly what you owe, but not a dime more. The rich just use the loopholes in the tax code to their advantage. Perfectly legal. They just do it differently than most employees.

This all became crystal clear to me when I read a book by Robert Kiyosaki entitled "The Cashflow

Quadrant."

The author clearly defines the four quadrants that most of us work within -- the 'E' quadrant, which is the employee, the 'S' quadrant, which is the self-employed person, the 'B' quadrant, which is the business owner, and the 'I' quadrant, which is the Investor quadrant.

E's have very little to no control over how much they pay in taxes, while the other quadrants have a much greater control over how much they pay.

To make a long-story bearable, what you must do to begin limiting the amount you pay in taxes is start a business (if even part-time) that allows you to write off some of your everyday expenses as business expenses.

As an example, early on in the course I mentioned that you could be buying things on Craigslist and then turning around and reselling them for a profit. Well, if that were a formalized "business", then you could pay for a number of the ordinary and necessary business expenses that go with it -- things like vehicle or mileage expenses, your computer, your internet, that digital camera you just bought, your cell phone bill, etc. All of these are necessary components to making this business run.

To do this, it's necessary to have a checking account separate from your personal accounts. It can be in your name with a dba (doing business as) followed by your business name. Make it something that is all-inclusive like J. Smith Enterprises.

Some tax prep folk will tell you that what you're doing is a hobby and not a business, but the definition of a business per the IRS is having the intent to show profit.

The best way we know to do that is to keep great records for your business. So you don't show a profit for 3 years ... that doesn't change the fact you have intent to show profit.

I'm going to pull back just a bit here because you have a look on your face like I just took a caveman into Best Buy for the first time.

This is borderline advanced stuff, but at this point in the course, you've changed your mindset when it comes to money. Hopefully, you've realized that taking the tried and true path isn't always tried and true when it comes to retiring early.

Here's the mission for this chapter: At the very least, consider what your business would be if you had one. From the beginning, my goal was to get you beginning to think like an entrepreneur and this is an exercise to stretch that muscle.

If you had a business, what is the name and what would you do to make money?

Keep in mind, this is something that you'd probably do on the side in addition to your regular job.

And, if you're really inspired to do something:
1. Pick up a copy of The Cashflow Quadrant by Robert Kiyosaki.
2. Start listening to podcasts like Smart Passive Income and Mixergy on iTunes.

And just so you know ... I don't think you look anything like a caveman.

Your Mission!

For Chapter 25, your mission is to at the very least, consider what your business would be if you had one. From the beginning, my goal was to get you beginning to think like an entrepreneur and this is an exercise to stretch that muscle.

Chapter 26
Get Paid What You're Worth

:: LESSON 26

Hola! You are going to think I have split-personality disorder when you start reading this email.

I think you're worth more than what you're making at work. Don't you?

In the last chapter, I was all about you starting a business and in this chapter, I'm all about you making more money in the job that you're in.

There is some method to my madness...

When you start thinking about how you'd make money on the side, sometimes you begin to realize that you're not paid the kind of money that you'd like to make. Sometimes, people realize that they can make some incredible part-time money and they'd like to make more at work to balance things out.

My dad gave me some dead-simple advice when I first started out in the working world. I was interviewing with a company and we were in the salary negotiation phase. When I told him that the manager I was interviewing with suggested that we revisit the salary in 6 months, my dad said, "there are two times when it's advantageous to negotiate salary, when you're coming and when you're going."

Before you go and threaten to quit your job, the reason I'm telling you this is most people don't know how to negotiate their salaries at the beginning and then fall short throughout their working life because they didn't negotiate high enough or often enough.

Your mission is going to be mapping out a salary review conversation with your supervisor to see if we can pull some more dough out of the company that you are working so diligently for.

There are a couple of secrets to salary negotiations working in your favor.

Number one, you want to do a considerable amount of research. The best places to do salary research would be www.salary.com and www.glassdoor.com. Do a search for your position, your company, your city and state, and any other search characteristic you can think of.

Your goal here is not to find out what Jerry in the corner office makes, but instead what Gary, who has your position at the company across town, makes.

Compare apples to apples, then decide if you're at the median, above, or below.

The second secret is to prepare a case for why you deserve to make more money. Come with very factual information about what you've accomplished, projects you've assisted on, and production that's come as a result of your efforts.

Focus on the details like productivity, efficiency, communication, cost-savings, sales ... anything that makes them think they'd be foolish not to give you more money.

Now, here's the kicker—you have to deserve it. If your track record at work isn't stellar, going in and asking for more money may get you laughed right out of the place.

Remember the movie Office Space?

"We hear you've been missing work, Peter."
"I wouldn't say I've been missing it, Bob."

When you're armed with these two main pieces of information -- the salary info and a detailed summary of your accomplishments -- then the next step is to schedule a time to go over your numbers with your supervisor.

Here's how to broach that subject:
Via Email:

Good afternoon, Jane.

Would you have 15 minutes at 4:00pm on Thursday or Friday to discuss my performance at work? I'd love some feedback and have some ideas to run by you.

Thanks!
--Stellar Employee

In Person:

Hey Jane, I was curious if you had a few minutes to spend together? It's been some time since my last performance review and I was hoping to share with you some of the progress I'm making with the silly string project. Does now work?

Once you're on the inside, the next step is to set the stage with your employer or supervisor. Here's how:

"I appreciate you carving out some time for me, Jane. One of the reasons I wanted to meet up was it's been some time since we went through my performance

with the company and I wanted to get your impression of how things are going."

At this point, let Jane do some talking and lead the conversation about your progress. It is now that you should be pulling out the comprehensive list of everything you've been up to. Once she's finished praising what a great job you did on the gigantic wax ball project, then you might interject with:

"Secondly, I wanted to share with you some information that I researched that suggest a salary review may be in order. According to my research, people in my position in companies of a similar size and in similar areas are making 16% more per year than I am. I'm super happy here, yet at the same time would like to think my performance is at least deserving of the median income or a little above for this position."

Then just shut your piehole. Salary negotiations are won and lost by who speaks first. There is a fair amount of information online about how to negotiate effectively, and if this is your weak spot, see if a co-worker, friend, or spouse will role-play with you to get you super comfortable with the ask.

Here's the rule of thumb, Super Saver -- Don't Ask, Don't Get.

I once heard a story of two millionaires walking down the street, when a homeless man asked them for $5. "I'm sorry, I don't have a five dollar bill, sir," said one of the men. The other told the beggar, "ask him if he has a fifty."

Life will certainly pay any price you ask of it. But you must ask.

Or as Yoda might say, "But ask you must."

May the force be with you.

Almost home...

Your Mission!

For Chapter 26, your mission is to do some research and find out what people in a similar position, similar company and location are getting paid. Figure out where you fit within those figures.

Compile a list of all the achievements you've completed at work and then book in a time to speak with your supervisor about your performance.

Chapter 27
Field Trip

:: LESSON 27

It's FIELD TRIP DAY! You remember how exciting field trips were in elementary school, right? I'd spend days daydreaming about getting on that bus in the middle of the morning and getting the heck out of dodge.

In this chapter, you get to revert back to your 4th grade self.

Our field trip is to the ... wait for it ... LIBRARY!

Before you go all buzz-kill on me, we're going to the library for a special mission. One of the keys to financial contentment, to living a life of abundance, and ultimately to retire with a fruity drink in one hand and a bottle of sunscreen in the other, is to begin to live the way the millionaires in your area do.

Contrary to popular belief, the millionaires in your area aren't driving sports cars and members of the country club. Instead, they're the folks next door who are driving Fords and Chevys that have been paid off for some time. They have modest homes, huge 401k plans, and live a less than extraordinary lifestyle.

I learned all of this in the same place you're going to learn it -- at the LIBRARY! As you've probably ascertained by this point, I've read a TON of financial books, but only a select few of them do I possess. The majority I went to the library and checked out. Just like you're going to do in this chapter.

The first book you're going in after is *"The Millionaire Next Door"* by Thomas Stanley and William Danko. Reading this incredible piece of research literature opened my eyes to the real truth behind some of my neighbors that were driving ultra expensive cars, owning second homes and working their tails off.

Just a few of the revelations you'll learn are:
- Ninety percent of millionaires live in homes valued below $1 million; 28.3% live in homes valued at $300,000 or less.
- On average, millionaires have a mortgage that is less than one-third of the value of their homes.
- If you really want to reduce your housing bill, join the 67,000 millionaires who live in mobile homes.

So, the field trip you're going on is a chance to step back to the days of yesteryear when you got REALLY excited about going into the library and coming out with an amazing book to read. (You once were really excited about going to the library, weren't you?)

Before the end of today, announce to your family and/or co-workers that you have an extremely important errand to run and get your financially content fanny over to the library to pick up *The Millionaire Next Door*!

You'll be glad you did ... who knows, we may even be millionaire neighbors someday.

When we drive our paid off Fords past one another, we can just smile and nod.

Your Mission!

For Chapter 27, your mission is to take a trip to the library and pick up a copy of *"The Millionaire Next Door"* by Thomas Stanley. Read it and learn...

Chapter 28
What to Do With Your Money

:: LESSON 28

You've done so well so far! Taking steps like these are no small feat, so congrats on making giant headway in your pursuit of financial contentment!

While I don't have access to your accounts or your FCF envelope, there's no way for me to see just how much you've put away so far. However, I have to imagine that with the saver skills you've acquired, your $1,000 account is fully funded (or well on it's way)!

So, the next step is to figure out what the next step is...

In the book you picked up in the last chapter (you DID pick up the book ... please tell me you picked up the book!) there is a story of a woman that decided she needed $5M in an account before retiring. On a salary of $90,000, she had already reached millionaire status because she knew where her money was going. In other words, she had a plan!

If you're plan up till now has been—have more

money at the end of the month instead of more month at the end of the money, that's a start. But what you may be missing is what to do with that money that's left over at the end of the month.

If you're like most of the folks you pass on a daily basis, ANY money left over usually gets spent at convenience stores, Target, or through shopping online at work (you've never done that, have you?).

The key is to get that money working for you somehow, somewhere!

Employ that money so it works harder than you do. Someday you'd like to retire and the key to making it to the beach phase of your life is to have your money working everyday the way you USED to.

The biggest hurdle you'll probably face, Super Saver, is deciding what to do with the extra money you now have. Remember, the $1,000 in a FCF was just the start. Now that you've ALWAYS got more money at the end of the month, deciding what to do with it becomes imperative.

You've got a few options, and my recommendation is to find someone to meet with to discuss them all. This could be a financial planner, a local advisor at a bank or credit union, or some super savvy uncle or aunt of yours that sends you a fifty dollar bill on your birthday.

Yes, we're talking stocks, bonds, mutual funds, real estate, gold & silver ... big kid investments that it's about time you learned about.

As a society, we're great at making money, but it's harder to keep it than to make it. And it's harder still to grow it than it is to keep it. But as you step up to the big kid table, these are the things you'll want to start learning about.

So, your mission for this chapter is to find someone that you can meet with to discuss what the future of your money looks like. Ask around those you trust for a referral to a great financial planner and set the appointment.

Your goal is just to get the ball rolling!

I'm not suggesting making sweeping changes just yet, but begin the process of paying attention to your money.

I've found that the more attention I paid to something, the better I do at it.

Where attention goes, energy flows, and results show.

That's some serious law of (money) attraction goodness.

Fishing with dynamite, KA-BOOM...

Your Mission!

For Chapter 28, your mission is to find someone that you can meet with to discuss what the future of your money looks like. Ask around those you trust for a referral to a great financial planner and set the appointment.

Your goal is just to get the ball rolling!

Chapter 29
The Grand Plan

:: LESSON 29

You have come so far and are so close to reaching the end of your money lessons ... PSYCHE!

This journey you've embarked on is not a temporary fix, but hopefully a long-lasting walk through the financial contentment forest.

It's said that businesses in Japan don't have a 5 or 10 year business plan but a 100 year plan or longer. Can you imagine seeing things out that far?

I hope you can, because I'm about to ask you to.

Chapter 29's assignment is to map out what the next 5 years, 10 years, 20 years, 50 years and if you are so bold, 100 years has in store for you financially.

I can almost hear the thoughts you're having right now — "100 years? That's absurd, I won't live to be past 110 anyway." Or something to that effect...

The critical Grand Plan you're creating is for the

immediate 5, 10 & 20 years. If you decide to go out even farther, you're mapping out what your family's finances will do in the future.

Consider it the Rockefeller Plan — after all, you don't become a family as wealthy as the Rockefeller's by just cruising along aimlessly. The senior Mr. John D. Rockefeller most definitely had a plan in mind for his family empire, and I'd say they've done pretty well!

To create the Grand Plan, begin by asking yourself a few questions:

1. What will life be like for me in 5 years? (10, 20 etc.)
2. How much will I need to have in investments to live the way I imagine?
3. My financial empire building team will consist of...
4. I've focused on building my net worth by...
5. In order to reach my 5, 10 & 20 year goals, I've done the following things consistently...
6. My net worth in 5 years will be... (and 10 & 20)

The document you're creating should become a living, breathing piece of art that you return to, modify, and live from for the foreseeable future.

It's said that it takes two generations to create a Rockefeller type fortune. The real question is, are you generation #1 or generation #2?

Without a solid game plan, a vision for the future, and consistent action you're likely to go down a path that doesn't get you closer to your ultimate goals but considerably farther away — and quite frankly, I'd like to see you on the same path I'm on several years from now.

It's the path that's full of fun times, good food, great vacations, luxurious seaweed and mud body wrap treatments...

Mmm, body wraps...

Your Mission!

For Chapter 29, your mission is to map out what the next 5, 10 & 20 years look like when it comes to your finances.

Create a living, breathing document that describes what life will be like, how much you'll have in savings and investments, and how you're going to get there.

This is your Rockefeller Plan. The guidebook to you achieving your greatest financial goals in life.

Something magical happens when you write down your greatest goals and review them regularly. So get crackin'!

Chapter 30
Celebrate Wins and Never Give Up

:: LESSON 30

I want to personally congratulate you for making it through the 30 Days To $1K Financial Contentment Course.

Did you know that the average college graduate only reads 0.9 books a year? Not even one entire book! The fact that you're reading the final chapter means that you are seriously above average! [cheers, shouting, whoops and hollers.]

If you've followed the coursework and lessons throughout the book, then you've achieved a greater level of financial contentment than you had previously. You are quickly on your way to becoming a financial ninja — I'd say at least an orange belt at this point!

It's time to celebrate some of the wins you've had along the way. For some people, saving money is an incredibly difficult thing to do. Literally having to reprogram their money mindset just to begin squirrelling away ANY amount. The fact that you are now becoming more hard-wired to do this is a

HUGE win and something you should celebrate.

You have down-sized some of the "stuff" that was keeping your money energy blocked. That's a major win as long as you keep the mindset of less is more until your cup runneth over with savings and investments.

Small holes sink great ships, and the fact that you've begun filling in all of those small holes is another HUGE win. You now know how to go about minimizing expenses and maximizing the money you make.

You've tackled the dreaded customer service rep phone calls and now think nothing of calling a service provider and giving them the run-around they usually give you. As my friend Charlie Sheen would say, "WINNING!"

So take a moment to celebrate your successes and the overall change in mindset and behavior you've experienced through this book. You deserve it ... it's hard work.

Then, realize that this is a process of continuous improvement. You've just scratched the surface when it comes to handling money and the 30 Days To $1K course has laid a foundation for you to become even more money savvy. Never give up on your path to acquiring wealth, success, fulfillment and happiness.

Today's assignment is simple: Write down all of the things you're proud of yourself for doing through the course of this book.

Contemplate how you've changed, what's different in your financial life, and how you're going to continue changing through the next several weeks, months and years.

Go you!

Your Mission!

For Chapter 30, your mission is to celebrate the wins that you've experienced through the course of this book. Make an exhaustive list of everything you've accomplished, what you've saved, how uncluttered your space is, and how great it feels to have a Grand Plan.

Be reflective as you do this, asking yourself "What else can I learn from this?"

Then, decide that you'll never give up on the path to financial contentment.

I believe in you!

Chapter 31
One Final Word

IT IS my sincerest hope that you enjoyed the process that this book took you through. While I have a passion for having fun in life, my greatest passion is helping people release themselves from the bonds of negative and limited thinking in order to Live A Bigger Life!

That starts with mastering your money.

I'll leave you with a quote from Napoleon Hill that hangs in my office as a constant reminder:

"Having definiteness of purpose in acquiring wealth is essential to it's acquisition".

May you continue on this path of financial contentment for years to come and share the gift of financial education with everyone you love!

About the Author

First and foremost, I'm a Dad and a Husband. My lifelong goal is to build a bigger life that sustains health, joy and happiness for me, my wife, and my kids. The second thing you must know is I'm a financial literacy junkie. I've found that those who are able to best make, manage, save, and invest their money are profoundly happier and more content with their lives.

The Official Stuff...

Adam Carroll is quickly being recognized as one of the top transformational trainers in the country. Having presented at over 500 colleges and Universities nationwide, hundreds of leadership symposiums, and countless local and regional organizations, Adam Carroll's message of *Building A Bigger Life, Not a Bigger Lifestyle* has been heard by over 200,000+ people.

In early 2014, Adam successfully crowd-funded a documentary on student loan debt, raising nearly $70,000 in 45 days. The film, *Broke Busted & Disgusted* is due out in the first half of this year (sign up here to get notified once it's live!) and is already garnering critical acclaim after Adam's TEDx talk at UW Milwaukee in September 2014. The mission of the film is to start a national debate about changing the way we fund college and not crippling 20-somethings with mountains of debt.

In an attempt to stop the problem before it starts, Adam's book Winning The Money Game, and corresponding curriculum, are being used in high schools and colleges as a financial literacy supplement. Students and educators are calling it a "game-changer" when it comes to handling money.

Also in 2014, Adam completed a 'Train the Trainer' program with Jack Canfield, author of *The Success Principles, The Aladdin Factor, The Power of Focus*, and the enormously popular *Chicken Soup For The Soul* book series. Adam's work with Jack and the 60+ transformational trainers continues to evolve and appear in his Build A Bigger Life Podcast and retreat events.

You can connect with Adam here:
- Twitter: https://twitter.com/AdamCarroll
- Facebook: https://www.facebook.com/AdamSpeaks
- YouTube: http://www.youtube.com/adamcarrollspeaks
- Email: adam@adamspeaks.com

Can you help?

If you liked this book and it was helpful to you, could you PLEASE leave a review on Amazon?

Simply visit http://amzn.to/1I4JOpY to leave your honest feedback!

Reviews are really important to the success of a book - so if you like (or don't like!) what you've read, PLEASE take 2 minutes to leave your honest review - I really appreciate it.